60 Credit Score & Credit Tips!

The book was created to provide information from a topic that is covered in the material. This book is sold with the understanding the publisher is not engaged in rendering nor responsible for any legal or accounting services fees of any kind. If you are unclear about the information, seek legal counsel or other professional advice.

This book was created in the United States of America.

ISBN 978-1-365-44200-1

First Edition

60 Credit Score & Credit Tips!

Contents

Introduction

This book was created to provide information about credit scores. To give you quick tips that you can review very quickly and implement right away.

When I decided to create this book. I wanted to provide helpful information that could be used immediately.

Working with many customers over the years realizing that people want access to information quick These are very helpful tips that are powerful and straight to the point.

This book was developed to help provide understanding of how credit scores are used. This is a great resource to use. Remember these tips are just the beginning of learning about credit scores and credit. Enjoy!

Understanding credit scores can
change your life!

Credit scores determine loan
qualifications.

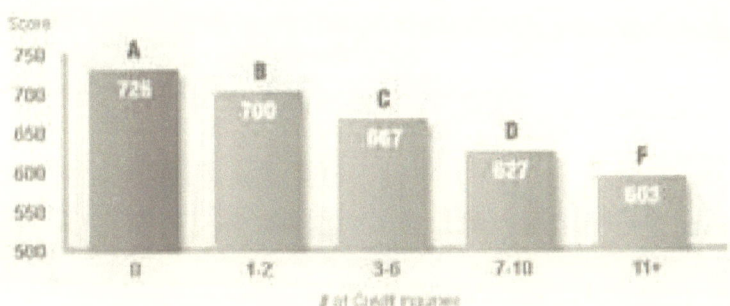

Credit scores are managed by credit
bureaus.

We have three credit bureaus that
manage our credit scores.

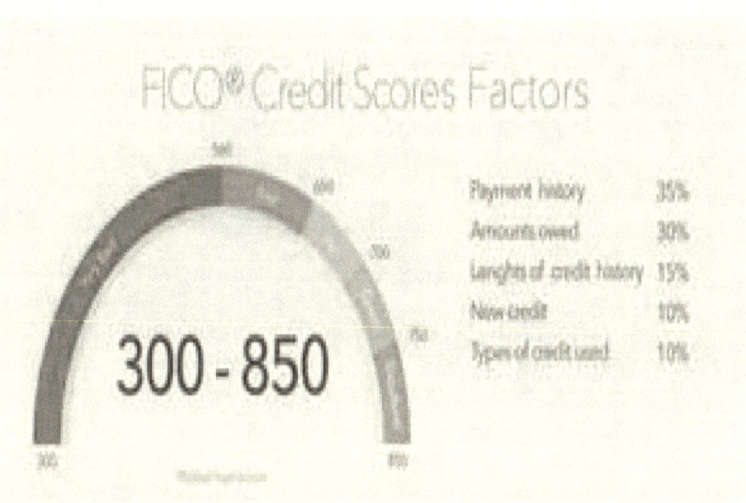

FICO® Credit Scores Factors

Payment history	35%
Amounts owed	30%
Lenghts of credit history	15%
New credit	10%
Types of credit used	10%

300 - 850

Credit scores are made up of formulas.

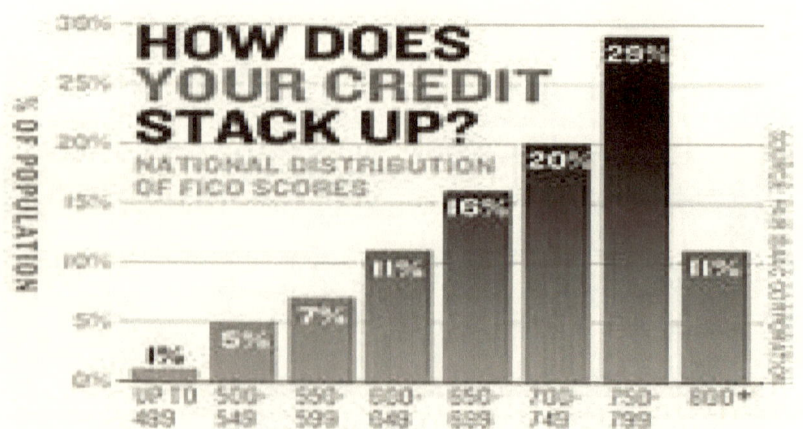

Credit scoring can vary from each credit bureau.

Credit scoring can vary from lender to lender.

The middle credit score determines
your loan terms.

Credit Score Range

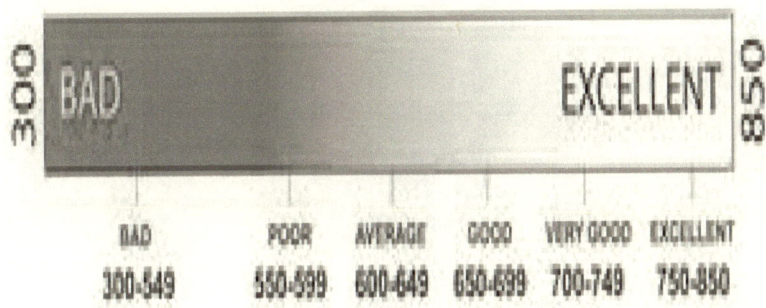

Credit scores can range from 300 to 850.

Poor credit scores range from 300 to 550.

Below average credit scores can range from 550 to 619.

Good credit scores can range from 620
to 650.

Excellent credit scores can range from
700 to 850.

Lenders use scoring methods to determine loan approval.

The 5 Key Contributors of Your Credit Score

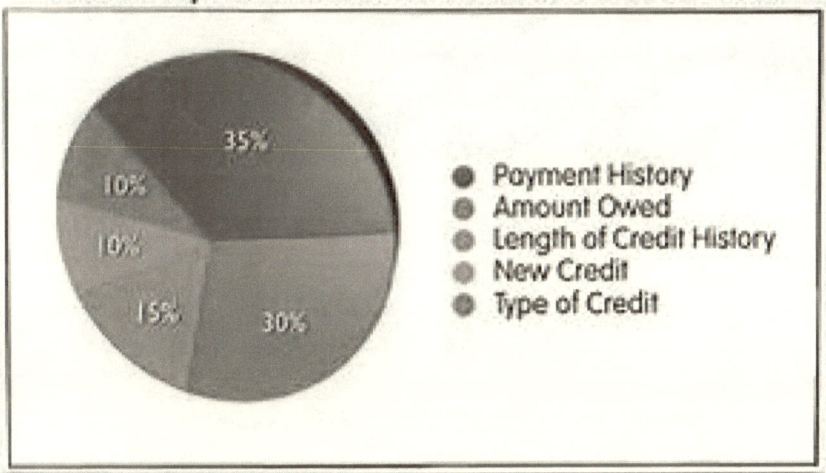

- Payment History
- Amount Owed
- Length of Credit History
- New Credit
- Type of Credit

35% of your credit scoring is
determined by how you make payments
over time.

30% of your credit scoring is
determined by how much you owe.

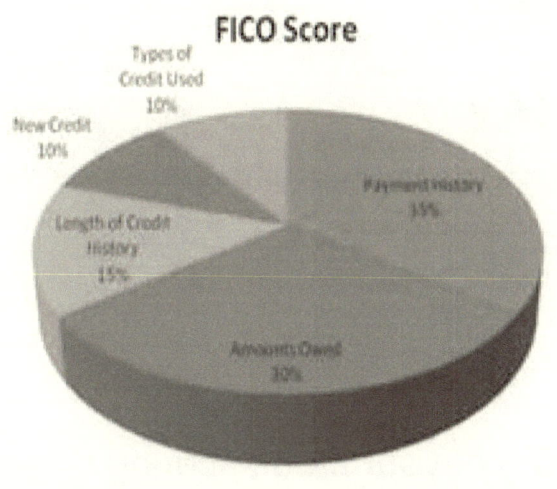

FICO Score

- Types of Credit Used 10%
- New Credit 10%
- Length of Credit History 15%
- Payment History 35%
- Amounts Owed 30%

15% of your credit scoring is determined by the length of your credit history.

10% of your credit scoring is determined by the type of accounts opened.

_____
_____
_____
_____
_____
_____
_____
_____
_____
_____
_____
_____
_____

10% of my credit scoring is determined
by any new credit opened.

Your credit scores can be affected
by your spending habits.

Your credit scores can be affected by
closing old accounts.

CREDIT INQUIRIES 101

Your credit score can change by too many credit inquires in a twelve month period.

Utilizing all of your available credit can affect your credit scores.

Removing bad accounts that are
more then ten years old.

What may work for someone else
may not work for your scores.

Not paying your bills on time can
affect your credit scores.

Opening too many credit cards at one
time can affect your credit score.

Judgements can affect your credit
scores negatively.

Bankruptcies can affect your credit
scores negatively.

Evictions can affect your credit
scores negatively.

Foreclosures can affect your credit scores negatively.

Repossessions can effect your credit
scores negatively.

Tax liens can affect your credit scores negatively.

Poor credit scores can cost you lots of money over time

Poor credit scores can cause denied
loan request.

Poor credit scores can cause denied
credit card loans.

_____
_____
_____
_____
_____
_____
_____
_____
_____
_____
_____
_____
_____
_____

Poor credit scores can cause you to have higher loan rates for an auto purchase.

Poor credit scores can cause you to
pay more money on a home loan.

_____
_____
_____
_____
_____
_____
_____
_____
_____
_____
_____
_____
_____
_____
_____
_____
_____

Your name is listed on your credit
report.

Hire a professional if you can not figure
out how to repair your credit scores.

Your credit report list your address.

Your credit report list your telephone number.

_____
_____
_____
_____
_____
_____
_____
_____
_____
_____
_____
_____
_____
_____
_____

Your credit report list your employer company name.

Your credit report list your martial
status.

_____
_____
_____
_____
_____
_____
_____
_____
_____
_____
_____
_____
_____
_____
_____
_____

Your credit report list your creditor names.

Your credit report list how much money
you owe to your creditors.

Your credit report list how long your
accounts have been opened.

Your credit report list any student loans
owed.

Your credit report list the balances of all
loans that you owe.

Your credit report list the dates of all accounts that were closed.

Your credit report list the date when all
of your account were opened.

Your credit report list your credit scores.

Your credit report list old debts that
were not paid.

Your credit report list how much you
pay each month towards your accounts.

Your credit report list your social
security number.

Your credit report tracks the history of every lender that you take out a loan with.

Your credit report tracks a history of every loan company that you sign a loan agreement with.

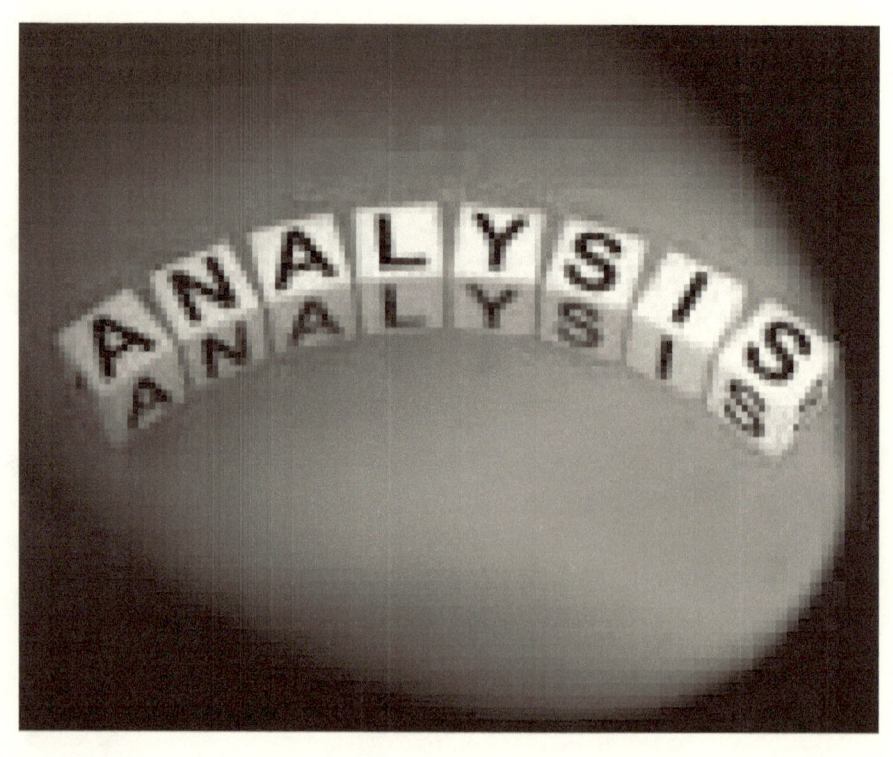

You can pull a copy of your credit report
annually for free.

Some credit repair companies offer a
free consultation.

Credit scores are a very important part
of your life.

www.ingramcontent.com/pod-product-compliance
Lightning Source LLC
Chambersburg PA
CBHW021911170526
45157CB00005B/2040